Pacific Grove

California Coast

California Coast

photography by David Muench
text by Jerry Cohen

RAND McNALLY & COMPANY
Chicago · New York · San Francisco

◀ Santa Barbara coast

Map of California

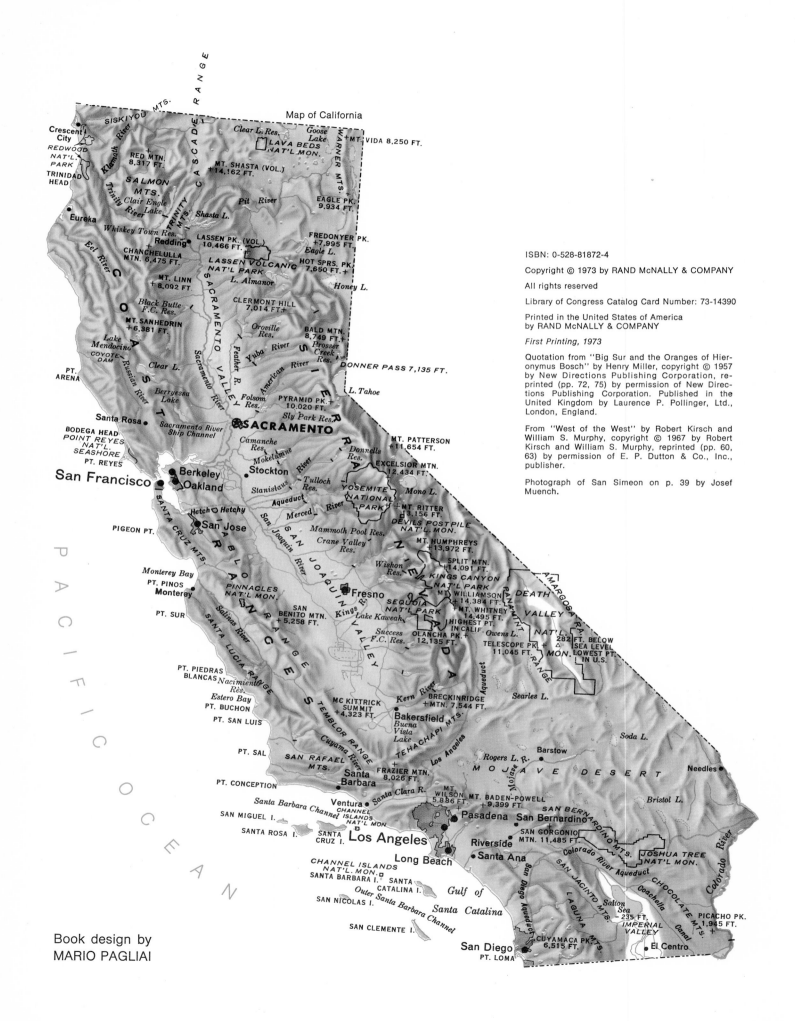

ISBN: 0-528-81872-4

Copyright © 1973 by RAND McNALLY & COMPANY

All rights reserved

Library of Congress Catalog Card Number: 73-14390

Printed in the United States of America
by RAND McNALLY & COMPANY

First Printing, 1973

Quotation from ''Big Sur and the Oranges of Hier-
onymus Bosch'' by Henry Miller, copyright © 1957
by New Directions Publishing Corporation, reprinted (pp. 72, 75) by permission of New Directions Publishing Corporation. Published in the
United Kingdom by Laurence P. Pollinger, Ltd.,
London, England.

From ''West of the West'' by Robert Kirsch and
William S. Murphy, copyright © 1967 by Robert
Kirsch and William S. Murphy, reprinted (pp. 60,
63) by permission of E. P. Dutton & Co., Inc.,
publisher.

Photograph of San Simeon on p. 39 by Josef
Muench.

Book design by
MARIO PAGLIAI

California Coast

BITS AND PIECES, colonnades and esplanades, capes, crooks, and crevices of that wondrous wedding of land and sea—the California coast—have been likened to all sorts of elsewhere places. But, in truth, the California coast, a serpentine 1,200 miles of jeweled beach and forbidding bluff, is a nowhere-else place—a unique shelf of scenic diversity defined by the ocean on one side and the sometimes snow-peaked Coast Ranges on the other. Moreover, each part of this uneven shoreline is a marvel unto itself.

The dissimilar California littoral encompasses the subtropical beachlands of the south coast, dotted with palm groves and caressed by mild ocean currents, and the roaring surf and fog-shrouded, conifer-forested capes of the north coast. As it winds along, it sometimes flattens into populous plains and valleys, where rise its cities. At other times, it shrinks to narrow defiles between sea and bleak headland, where isolated villages, or a lone dwelling or two, dangle perilously from bluff and above river slough.

This shoreline is home to nearly 17 million of California's approximately 19 million residents. Half of that 17 million, perhaps, reside in the dense urban centers of Los Angeles, San Diego, and San Francisco and their environs. The other half live in resort cities such as Newport Beach, Santa Barbara, Monterey, Half Moon Bay, and Jenner; in affluent La Jolla, Balboa, Carmel, Shelter Cove, and Trinidad; in the workaday towns of National City, Long Beach, Daly City, Fort Bragg, Eureka, and Crescent City.

These California coast people work and play in a contrast of climates, which belies the notion held by many other Americans that California—its fabled coast especially—is always temperate, always sun-spangled. It is true that summer rainfall is not a common phenomenon throughout most of the state. It also is true that there is a small ribbon of coast, southern California's, which generally remains undisturbed by climatic uproar. It also is fact that the shoreline's moistness and warmth make for the most uniform temperatures in the country.

But because the California shore extends through nearly ten degrees of latitude, dips and ascends to extremes of elevation, and is subject to the caprices of ocean currents, the state's coastal weather—for the most part—disallows monotony. And when Nature does play tricks there, she makes a spectacle of herself.

The annual rate of rainfall diminishes appreciably from north to south. In San Diego, it averages only about nine inches each year. But at the village of Honeydew, situated amid Humboldt County's soaring redwoods, it reached a record annual high of almost 200 inches one year.

Now what about that California sunshine, so publicized in song and story, so sacred to chamber of commerce and tourist bureau brochure? It's there—make no mistake about that, and in great plenitude. The mean annual amount of sunshine along the coast corresponds to the quantity of rainfall—only in reverse—and varies just as widely. For instance, the sun shines slightly less than 50 percent of the time at Eureka in wet Humboldt County but about 90 percent along the southern coast, where the average is more than 3,000 hours of sunshine annually, compared with 2,200 in Eureka. The line of demarcation for sunshine, or lack of it, along the coast is the San Francisco Bay Area, north of which it dwindles rapidly.

But it is the Pacific Ocean—gently lapping the shore at times, recklessly cannonading it at others—that gives the California coast its matchless character. George R. Stewart once spoke of its "dominating presence," and he wrote that it "not only produces the much admired scenery of surf-pounded beaches, cliff-faced headlands and offshore rocks—but it also insures that, by and large, the coastal region is cooler and more moist than the regions inland."

But all does not sparkle along the magic shoreline of the California coast. There is man-made blight. And, sometimes, there is natural horror—fire . . . flood . . . earthquake. Sometimes man's blight is deceptive, disguised as rich men's homes crowded tight against one another along the oceanfront, forming a barrier that walls off the view of the sea. Sometimes the blight results from the sprawl of industry, which pollutes the air and produces noise that drowns the sounds of the surf. Sometimes the blight is deliberate, where developers erect residential subdivisions—with oceanic names—that stretch antenna-topped down to the shore.

The creation in 1972's November election of one statewide and six regional commissions to "preserve, protect and, where possible, to restore" the California coastline offers high hope that man-made blight will be halted. What the agencies come up with will be presented to the legislature in 1976. Meantime, the commissions have some unprecedented powers, one of which permits them to regulate development within 1,000 yards of the Pacific.

But even if man's abuse of the coast is halted and, to an extent, repaired, Nature will remain contentious as always.

Fire . . . . .

During the dry months of summer and fall, southern California, right down to the shoreline, becomes a roaster. Residents, especially those on parched canyon hillsides, live in dread of a carelessly handled cigarette or negligently discarded match. And when the normal air currents from the west change and a peculiarly southern California hazard known as the Santa Ana Winds begin to whine across the mountains from burning deserts, sprinklers go on everywhere. Santa Ana gusts reach up to 100 miles an hour and turn brushfires, which suddenly seem to break out everywhere in southern California, into potentials for fiery disaster.

Flood . . . . .

When heavy rain comes, and it comes in the southern California winter, it is often fraught with the seeds of catastrophe because of the very fires which earlier have ravished hillside and canyon. That's because its twin is mud slide. Torrents simply carry away the land that has been stripped of its vegetation by flame. Slime and water knock the props from under homes or simply fill every room with goo. Swollen waters rush along, then overflow normally dry streambeds, and entire neighborhoods disintegrate into a soggy, muddy mess.

Earthquake . . . . .

California, as even the least-informed person must certainly know, is earthquake country. Literally thousands of minor jolts each year shake some slice of the California coast or some other part of the state, which sits atop a faulty, unstable piece of fragile earth crust. At the very least perhaps 500 annually are felt by some residents. Noticeable damage from these is rare. But a killer quake did rend the Los Angeles area in 1971, causing deaths and extensive property damage.

Geologists and seismologists look askance today at the skyscrapers rising at an ever-increasing rate in the state's major cities. Builders claim they have made their big-city high rises, if not quakeproof, at least temblor-resistant. But the real test—the monster slippage along a fault in the earth's crust that most experts expect someday—is yet to come.

Yet no one who counts himself a true California coast person would trade the myriad delights of living where he does for such a mundane consideration as mere safety.

WHERE IT ALL BEGINS, this sometime knobby, sometime honeycombed, 1,200-mile reach of land wedded to water, lies in the eye of the beholder. It starts either north or south, depending on one's allegiance.

Most northern Californians, I have no doubt, would maintain that it begins where the state abuts its northern neighbor, lush Oregon. Being a southern Californian, I advance the contrary view.

For me, the California coast journeys northward from the outskirts of a dreary, dusty Mexican city of sin, poverty, and tourism that is trying to shed a reputation acquired during a lurid past and become respectable. If effort reaps reward, Tijuana may just do that. Which is a damn shame in the minds of those who appreciate fleshpots as long as they are confined to the other fellow's backyard.

Here, at the extreme southwestern tip of the United States, a serene and splendid beach spirals below a low bluff on which stands a fourteen-foot, white-marble obelisk marking the International Boundary.

Directly north of the 1851 boundary monument, the mesa dips to low marshy land which, after perhaps half a dozen miles, encounters the southerly arm of magnificent San Diego Bay, the southwesternmost harbor of the continental United States.

Despite its virgin character, the Pacific face below the gentle bluff was, not all that long ago, one of the most unvisited beaches in southern California. But no longer. Although still unspoiled, it now is part of a spanking-new gem in the state park system that encompasses more than a mile of beachfront, plus salt marsh and a splendid estuary which host a dazzling bouquet of birdlife. Shore birds and sea birds are joined here by inland species from the purple hills of

Mexico to the south and from the San Diego County backcountry to the east. The 372 acres of Border Field State Park were transferred to California by the U.S. government (the area had been a naval property called Border Field).

Up past Imperial Beach, just to the north, a shillelagh-shaped sandspit extends between ocean and bay. The southern end of this walking-stick thrust of low-lying land about ten miles long is connected with the mainland at Imperial Beach. The knob of the spit is what popularly is known as Coronado Island, which really is not an island at all, you see, and is only partially occupied by the fetching city of Coronado, the remainder being part of the U.S. Navy's ubiquitous presence in the San Diego area.

The slender peninsula is what primarily shields the quiet waters of the twenty-two-square-mile bay, providing shelter from the ocean's surges for a hodgepodge of vessels of all sizes and shapes. Point Loma, a headland hooking down from the north, is the bay's other protecting arm.

The ocean side of the peninsula is steep and gleams with silvery bits of a trillion shells, from whence has come its name: the Silver Strand, a state beach.

The jewel of Coronado Island reposes like some grande dame just to the north of the strand. It is the Hotel Del Coronado, a Victorian marvel which opened in 1888 and whose five stories of turrets and cupolas, balconies and dormer windows have heard the footfalls of presidents and kings.

Once, to reach Coronado from the San Diego mainland, one took one of the majestic old ferries that ran with the constancy of a railroader's watch. Now, a graceful, high-arcing bridge does the job. Motorists have a superb view, 200 feet above water, of the bustle of the bay—busy wharves, giant aircraft carriers, the West Coast's largest tuna fleet, the navy's mothball armada—or, at night, the San Diego skyline twinkling like a gemmed tiara.

Lighthouse at Point Loma

Mission San Diego de Alcalá

Torrey Pines State Reserve

AN DIEGO BAY, one of the most hospitable natural harbors anywhere, was discovered in 1542 by Juan Rodríguez Cabrillo, a Portuguese explorer working for Spain. Ever since, the city which grew up around it has cherished, like a prized heirloom, its Spanish patrimony and its ties as well to the nation of which it once was part, Mexico. From 1825 to 1830, San Diego served as the unofficial capital of Mexico's Alta California. (The governor, it seems, simply preferred the climate to that of Monterey, the official capital.)

In 1769 Father Junípero Serra arrived to found the Mission San Diego de Alcalá, along with a presidio and pueblo. It was the first of many he established which became settlements around which grew other great California cities, including San Francisco (1776). The old mission still stands in what one writer called a state of "dignified decay" in Old Town, about four miles northwest of modern downtown San Diego.

La Jolla coast

San Diego today is quite unlike its two formidable rivals—Los Angeles and San Francisco—in many respects. It is cleaner and less congested, its downtown is orderly and relatively quiet, with little radical departure in architecture. Although metropolitan San Diego has a population of about 1½ million, the city still has a small-town aura about it. San Diego's serenity is marvelously sensed at twilight when one looks back across the bay from the Old Lighthouse atop Point Loma, now a part of Cabrillo National Monument—a view the *Encyclopaedia Britannica* has described as one of the three most beautiful marine panoramas in the world.

But above all, San Diego has an absolutely incomparable climate. It is the driest of the coastal cities, and the sun dominates everything else; it is not idle bombast when boosters refer to the bay as the "Harbor of the Sun." Morning clouds and sea breezes moderate temperatures even in summer, and the absence of frost not only makes for a year-round growing season but encourages San Diegans' enthusiasm for sports and outdoor living throughout all twelve months. Even the names of many San Diego neighborhoods and suburbs such as Ocean Beach, Mission Beach, and Pacific Beach—suggest an obsession with the leisure life.

Seven-mile-square aquatic Mission Bay Park is an alluring inland extension of these and other ocean playfields. Fifty-five million dollars in dredging and development created this pleasure world for San Diego residents and what has become a stunning motel- and hotel-rich resort for tourists, upon whose business no small piece of the San Diego economy depends. From Mission Bay's twenty-seven miles of palm-impaled shoreline, the stroller or lounger may observe almost any kind of water sport. Swimmers, water-skiers, and boatmen frolic on the site of what only a few years ago was a smelly expanse of mud flats, known to early explorers as False Bay because of the frequency with which their vessels mired in its muck.

Between here and Del Mar's fragrant eucalyptus trees about twenty miles north, swimmers and surfers come to ride the high, warm breakers off a series of white beaches, broken often by steep sandstone cliffs such as those at La Jolla and Torrey Pines Mesa.

This alternating sweep of broad sunny beach, cove, and abrupt cliffland generally persists along the coast all the way up to the forbidding stone ramparts of the Big Sur country.

The lower southern California shore, although unprotected, is a balmy

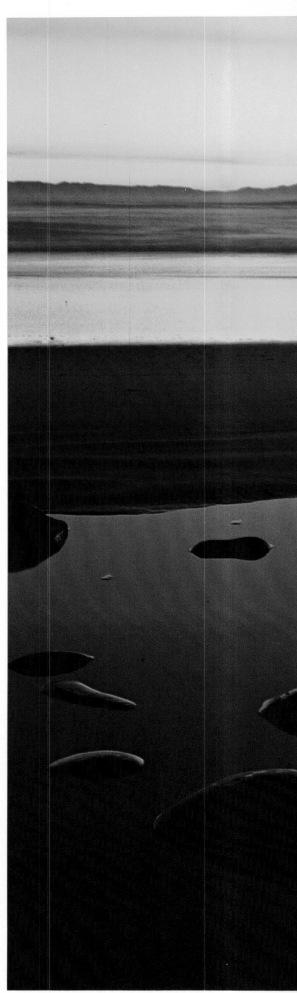

Tidal pools

Laguna Beach ▶

The *Queen Mary*, Long Beach

domain, except for occasional winter storms which sometimes bring rough seas, heavy swells, and violent winds. Fog descends upon it less frequently than might be expected; when the fog arrives, it does so most often at night and usually departs by midmorning.

But well-behaved though the surf normally is, where the waves meet sandstone bulwarks like those at La Jolla and Torrey Pines, they explode with awesome intent.

Consider La Jolla, that posh and captivating suburb of San Diego, where almost anyone would live if he could afford to, whose name is said to derive from a Spanish word—*joya*—that translates, fittingly, into "jewel," and which is the site of the University of California's Scripps Institution of Oceanography, renowned for its research into the mysteries of the sea.

The waves battering against La Jolla's bluffs over the centuries have sculptured rocky masterpieces. Most notable are the half-dozen grottoes piercing the cliffs around La Jolla Cove. Outside the seaside caves, five of which can be entered only from the ocean, scuba divers search for briny treasures. On the floors inside the caves, explorers of tidal pools poke around in the seawater

Newport Beach

Los Angeles

Civic Center mall, Los Angeles

Hollywood Hills

Point Vicente Lighthouse

Mission San Gabriel Arcángel

Coreopsis bloom, Point Mugu

Mission Santa Barbara

gardens, looking for the myriad prizes left behind by the ebbing tide.

Tidal pools are a joy of almost the entire California coast. Each is a whole universe in which, it has been said, small "animals" of the sea thrive, exhibiting habits "a good deal more bizarre, or comic, or miraculous than any human swimmer's." The performers in this saltwater circus are starfish and mussels, sea urchins and sea anemones, snails, clams and worms, crabs of all sorts, and even barnacles.

From La Jolla, the coast curves easterly ever so slightly to a high mesa known as Torrey Pines, because of the rare and twisted trees which grow there. On the sandstone face of the mesa are the exposed, gnarled root systems—relics of the Ice Age—of many of these pines, which grow only one place else: on off-shore Santa Rosa Island, more than 100 miles northwest. The roughly 2,500 survivors here are fiercely protected by conservationists, and the tough old trees deserve all this loving care, for theirs has been an epic stand against the same relentless ocean winds responsible for shaping their grotesque beauty. These trees have the longest and strongest needles of any pines in the world.

The same steady whip of air that has warped the pines has drawn an adventurous breed of man to the mesa. He is the daredevil glider pilot. Almost any weekend when the thermals are favorable, graceful sailplanes soar eaglelike on rising columns of air off the bluffs. Torrey Pines Mesa has become a world favorite among glider buffs.

The southern California coast from this point north is almost uninterrupted settlement, one exception being Camp Pendleton, the U.S. Marine Corps' sprawling military reservation. Occasionally, the marines set out in boats and return to shore by foot, slogging through the surf in training for amphibious assaults.

It is a seemly stretch of habitation, this one along the southern California coast. In the seaside towns of northern San Diego County, residents live much more in tune with the ocean than with the humming concrete ribbon of the eight-lane coastal freeway which winds, in most cases, slightly inland of each community.

They are towns with names like Del Mar, Solana Beach, Cardiff-by-the-Sea, Encinitas, Leucadia, Carlsbad, and Oceanside, which is just below the Camp Pendleton boundary. Along their domain run strings of white beach and mostly gentle bluffs whose shores are inhabited by all kinds of fishlife, including lobster and abalone, the latter being a pet prey of spearfishers.

And, of course, there is the running of the grunion, which may sound like a myth to newcomers to the Pacific shore but which is indeed for real. The grunion run is one of the great comic sights each year on some southern California beaches. On the nights when this occurs, and it is possible to tell in advance, men, women, and children descend on the sands where, quite literally, they are able to pick up with their hands the wriggly silvered creatures. This, in fact, is the only way to catch the half-foot-long fish because a law prohibits the use of nets. The run comes when the grunion squirm ashore to spawn during summer months, always on the second, third, and fourth nights after a full moon and always during a three-hour period following high tide. The lovely beach below Del Mar is a favorite of the grunion crowd, whose trusty tools are only a good flashlight and, as they say in football parlance of the best wide receivers, "good hands and good moves."

Del Mar itself is a tree-shaded resort town once famous for an exquisite old hotel popular with horse-fancying movie stars but now best known for its beautiful racetrack situated almost at seaside.

Carlsbad, about ten miles north, is a venerable town named after the Bohemian spa of Karlsbad (present-day Karlovy Vary in Czechoslovakia). The early settlers found a well with water having the same mineral content as the

Fremontia   Tree mallow

Santa Barbara

Lompoc

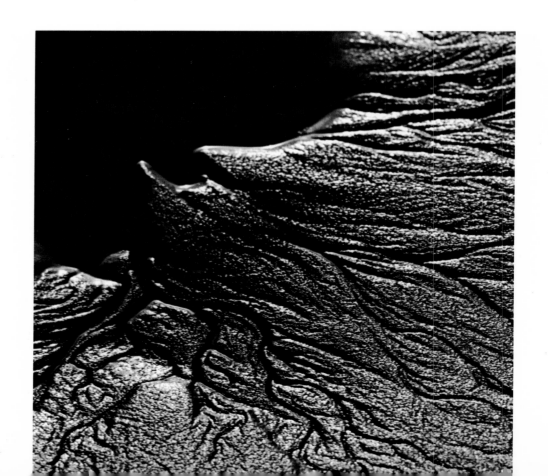

one in the European resort. The California Carlsbad today grows cut flowers and prizes a quaint little railroad station which opened in 1888 and is kept spick and span and freshly painted—even though the trains don't stop there anymore.

Booming Oceanside, which seems to grow bigger every year and is the city where Camp Pendleton's marines while away their leisure hours, also is a flower-raising center. During the growing months, anemone, ranunculus, and gladiolus enflame the Oceanside coast with a burst of color—pink and red, white and yellow, magenta and orange.

Sitting like a great half-buried basketball on a coastal bluff just within the northern boundary of 250,000-acre Camp Pendleton, which begins north of Oceanside and once was an old Spanish land-grant rancho, is the San Onofre Nuclear Generating Station. It is one of the few such nuclear-powered plants producing electricity for peacetime purposes and the object of frequent criticism by conservationists.

Just to the north is San Clemente, site of President Richard M. Nixon's Western White House and the most southerly town of the Orange County coast, a summertime mecca for vacationers from the Los Angeles metropolitan area.

San Clemente literally sparkles in the sun, or so it seems to a yachtsman sailing by or a motorist driving past. This is because of the still-prevailing and once almost-exclusive character of its homes and other buildings: whitewashed walls and red-tiled roofs.

From San Clemente, the shoreline climbs past Capistrano Beach, an adjunct to the old mission town of San Juan Capistrano, to a spot bold with rocky cliffs rising 200 feet above a sandy beach. This is historic Dana Point, named for Richard Henry Dana, Jr., author of the more than a century-and-a-quarter-old sailing classic, *Two Years Before the Mast*.

It was here in 1818 that the pirate Hippolyte de Bouchard anchored his fleet during a voyage of plunder down the California coast and raided the mission at San Juan Capistrano in the hills inland from the promontory.

And it was here a decade-and-a-half later that the brig *Pilgrim* out of Boston with Dana aboard reached a sheltered bight beneath the precipitous cliffs which today is known as Dana Cove. The *Pilgrim* moored just offshore to take on cargo from the mission: stiff, heavy cowhides which the rancheros hurled over the cliffs to the sands below. From there, Dana and his fellow crewmen

Mussels

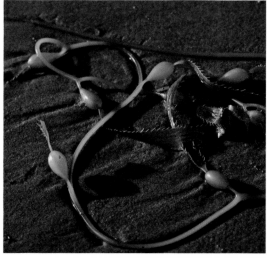

Kelp

carried the cargo on their heads aboard the brig which sat not too safely in the tossing waters of the cove.

Dana Point today is a handsome town growing, it seems, more populous by the day. Its streets have names that might have pleased Dana—like Street of the Copper Lantern and Street of the Amber Lantern. At the end of one, the Street of the Blue Lantern, sits a little cupola at the brink of the steep cliff, a sheer wall which Dana thought "perilous." It affords a spectacular panorama of the Pacific. Except for the modern bustle and the structures along the shore, which go largely unnoticed from that inspiring vista, the beauty of the setting is unchanged since Dana mused upon it and later wrote:

". . . there was a grandeur in everything around which gave a solemnity to the scene, a silence and solitariness which affected every part! Not a human being but ourselves for miles, and no sound heard but the pulsations of the great Pacific! and the great steep hill rising like a wall, and cutting us off from all the world, but the 'world of waters'!

Arroyo Burro Beach

Blue Ceanothus

Nojogui Falls

Live oak, Santa Ynez Valley

"Compared with the plain, dull sand-beach of the rest of the coast, this grandeur was as refreshing as a great rock in a weary land. . . ."

San Juan Capistrano Mission, with which the *Pilgrim* traded and which Bouchard raided, is three miles inland in the town of the same name. The original chapel has been restored. A much larger church built later was destroyed by an earthquake in 1812.

It has been called the most beautiful of all the California missions, and, of course, has been celebrated in song and story as the place "the swallows come back to." And it's true. The mission, great parts of it now a picturesque ruin, bids good-bye—so legend tells it—to the swallows on the name day of its patron saint, Saint John, each year in October only to await their faithful return every Saint Joseph's Day in March. Sometimes the birds' timetable is off a little, but rarely by more than a day or two, so the "miracle of the swallows" should not be examined too closely. An aged priest, once asked about "the miracle," commented, "Everything in life is a miracle." Then he sagely added that swallows almost everywhere in the world follow much the same migration pattern.

The hills above the old mission and others that rise northwestward from the coastline turn a ripe, golden yellow in summer. Running down from them between Dana Point and Laguna Beach, about six miles to the north, are deep and narrow arroyos which split the 40- to 100-foot-high cliffs and open onto coves and some fine white beaches.

The most extensive of the beaches forms the seaward wing of the blithe-spirited city of Laguna Beach, an arty haunt the year around but an absolute carnival of gaudy, touristy beachwear and bare, baked flesh, both male and female, young and old, during the summertime.

Laguna Beach is a long-established art colony that may have more studios and galleries per block than any place else on the Pacific coast. That's just maybe, since residents of La Jolla, Sausalito, and Mendocino might challenge this fact. However, Laguna alone can claim a long-running summer Festival of Arts which is a sellout every year.

From Laguna Beach to Newport Beach, the coast continues along the same smooth northwestward curve which began at La Jolla and is generally uninterrupted until the Palos Verdes Peninsula, a part of metropolitan Los Angeles, juts its bluffy jaw out into the ocean just beyond Long Beach. The six-mile stretch between Laguna Beach and Newport Beach is rocky and indented by a succession of coves.

Corona del Mar, another jewel of a town, looks down from a sea cliff to the entrance of swank Newport Bay, where an armada of between 7,000 and 8,000 small craft of every description, from commercial fisherman's dory, to rich man's yacht, to an imitation Chinese junk, bob at their moorings. Newport Bay is a web of channels, basins, and canals dredged in the mouth of a natural estuary which extends several miles into an inland lagoon. The harbor is protected from the sea by a three-mile-long sandspit, Balboa Peninsula. The 740-acre bay has a total water frontage of sixteen miles and is ornamented with exclusive residential islands, among which Lido Isle is the toniest. A fifty-foot waterfront lot on Lido might fetch close to $200,000.

Rich man's province though it may be, Newport Bay is home port also for a nonconformist gaggle of Portuguese-descended dory fishermen plying the same sea trade as their fathers and grandfathers before them. The hardy little band leaves for the deep seas before dawn, and when the dories return, the fishermen pull their flat-bottomed boats ashore and set up an open-air market on the beach cleaning and filleting what customers buy right on the spot.

Huntington Beach, half a dozen miles up the shore, calls itself the "Surfing Capital" of the nation—and with considerable justification.

Oceano coast

Morro Rock

Surfing is an absolute craze along the southern California coast, and it's popular even along northern beaches where no matter how chilly the seawater, it fails to daunt the hardy, wet-suited devotees of the sport, who tote their flat, missilelike boards down to the breakers. Even the beach at Crescent City, not far south of the Oregon border, attracts its share of surfing buffs.

The virtuoso does his surfing in an erect position and "hanging ten," meaning with all toes over the nose of the board. This requires mastery of the art, especially with the kind of surf found at such meccas of the sport as Huntington Beach. Other pet haunts of surfers include the beaches of San Diego County and Santa Monica Bay.

But if spilling breakers—waves on the verge of breaking for a great distance but which do not actually break until within a few feet of the shore—are a characteristic of Huntington Beach, so is its unmistakable, pungent aroma. The beach city and the approaches to it smell of oil, and a newcomer needs no explanation as to why. The area is forested with derricks briskly pumping petroleum from deep within the tidelands. At a clutch of places along the coast from Huntington Beach north to Santa Barbara, the presence of the oil industry is highly visible, but the greatest concentration of wells is in these two localities and on Terminal Island, in San Pedro Bay between Los Angeles and Long Beach and shared by the two cities.

THE ALMOST, but not quite, unbroken stretch of habitation that began along the shore north from San Diego continues to above Santa Barbara, but along the way it encompasses the southern California megalopolis, as some call it—the electric, muscular sprawl that is metropolitan Los Angeles. Here is nose-to-nose and wall-to-wall construction. Homes and commercial buildings contest for space on the shoreline, some separated from it for varying distances by the multilane Pacific Coast Highway.

Homeowners pack their residences as close to the water as the surf permits, just beyond reach of the highest tide where possible. Those who build on bluffs vie for the best view of the sea.

This coastal carapace of the vast city of Los Angeles first crooks gently in, hooks seaward again around the Palos Verdes Peninsula, curves back, then takes a sharp dash west from Santa Monica toward Port Hueneme. It is a coastal shelf which slopes so gradually to the sea that wide expanses of beach reduce the pounding surf to a lazy, gossamer froth, tempered to agreeable mildness by the warming ocean current which flows south from Point Conception.

While cliffs and rocks are abundant here, they do not dominate the shoreline. Thus, its miles of open strand are easily accessible and, on weekends, teem with humanity. Although fogs and mists occasionally surge in from the ocean, these most commonly persist, as the weather service is wont to say, only "during night and early morning hours." The sky usually clears by midmorning, leaving the air soft and balmy. By this time of day, however, within the great metropolis and its inland satellites, both air and sky are often already rank with smog.

Seen from the air, this coastal ribbon, extending close to eighty miles between Huntington Beach and Malibu, is a bric-a-brac of beach cities and towns, bays, and the colossal twin harbors of Los Angeles and Long Beach. Although the latter extend along the shoreline of San Pedro Bay, they were carved by man from slough and estuary. And "bay" really may not be a proper name for these waters since there is no natural harbor. This, of course, is a matter of rather subtle semantics, since other of the bays along this particular slice of coast were partially, at least, man-made too.

With rare exceptions, the city and town names identify their proximity to the water: Sunset Beach, Surfside, Seal Beach (just south of the Los Angeles County line), Redondo Beach, Hermosa Beach, Manhattan Beach, Venice, Ocean Park. Some like Torrance and Wilmington sound like old stick-in-the-

Pelicans

Big Sur

San Simeon

California poppies

Soledad Mission

muds. The bays have such names as Sunset, Anaheim, Alamitos, and Santa Monica. Santa Monica, of course, is also the name of a city, and a picture-postcard one it is too. Santa Monica, Long Beach, and possibly Malibu are the most quickly identified by nonresidents as coastal offshoots of Los Angeles.

After all that has been written about Los Angeles (call it "L.A.," if you will, and Angelenos are not offended—unlike San Franciscans, who resent the expression "Frisco"), one wonders what more can be said about the seething, tumultuous, ever-changing supercity that still defies definition. Well, certainly this at least: it *IS* most of the things said about it, yet again *IT IS NOT*. The exaggerations have been too gross, the good points, the graces too frequently ignored or overwhelmed by snide jest. A major contributor to the distortion may be the never-never land called Hollywood, which really is all make-believe. Hollywood is the fantasy of the movie industry, which grew from infancy in New York to affluent, flamboyant maturity in Los Angeles; it returned the compliment, the industry did, by making Los Angeles appear somewhat unreal too.

But it is true that Los Angeles does have all those backyard swimming pools and barbecues, all that smog, all those rush-hour-strangled freeways, all those kooks and way-out mystics. And all those pop-art buildings, most of them hangovers from the twenties and thirties when if anyone had heard the phrase pop art, he would have thought it a description for the design of a soft-drink bottle.

But Los Angeles also has great art and cultural complexes, the most recent being the new Music Center, which has three separate theaters. It also has superb colleges and universities, with velvety green campuses and tasteful buildings. Its athletic plants are known to sports-minded men and women all over the world, consistently fielding teams and heroes that merit celebrity. It has fine stores and parks and some of the best restaurants, not just in the United States, but in the world. As a city in which to eat, Los Angeles has been too easily dismissed, the claims of superiority for San Francisco, New York, and New Orleans notwithstanding.

The people who live here too are one of its great municipal assets. They are diverse, innovative, fairly aburst with energy, yet leisure loving. Los Angeles' population, despite the large number of retired persons who come here from other parts of the country, is a young one, with a median age below the national average. It is said that the typical married couple is two or three years younger than their counterparts elsewhere in the country, is better educated and has a higher income than the average American, and has 1.2 children, as compared to the national norm of 2.5. It is a highly mobile population, and as might be ex-

Little Sur River

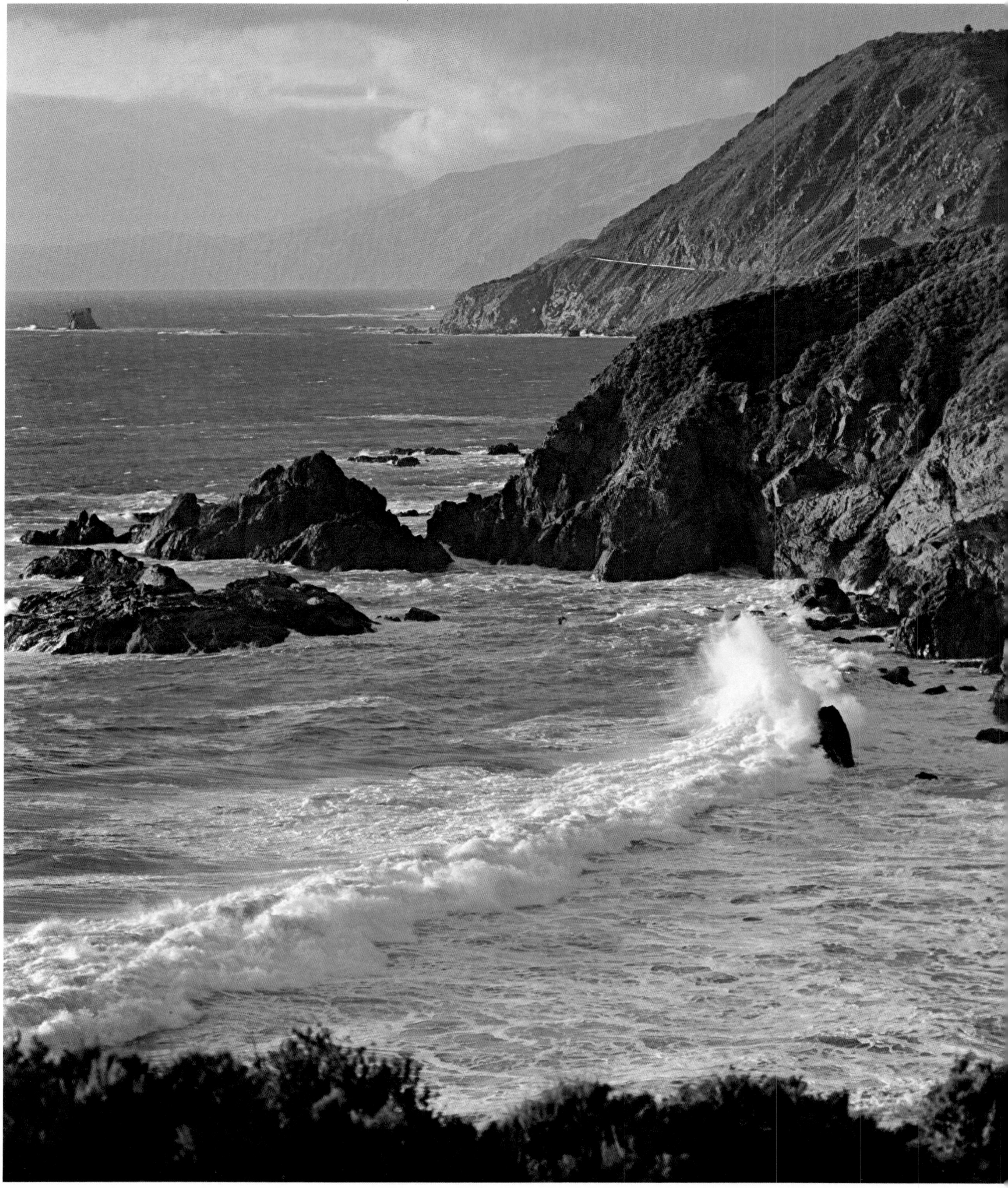

Point Sur

Big Sur coastline

pected, it owns 1.5 automobiles per family, half again as many as the average for the nation as a whole.

Beginning as a Spanish pueblo where the restored Old Plaza now stands, then recast first as a Mexican town and finally as a Yankee city, Los Angeles sprawls raggedly over a dry, alluvial plain from the base of the mountains to the sea. Here and there, a cord of hills or a fickle-dry watercourse interrupts the level monotony. Although the city boasts few elevations with memorable views, it has its moments. But it is no San Francisco or San Diego in that respect, and most of its beauties are man-wrought: sylvan parks, exquisitely landscaped residential neighborhoods, and broad boulevards.

However, its greatest lure, as it is elsewhere in most of southern California, is a climate that, for those who do not insist on four seasons, is inarguably almost ideal. The best times are the days when the marine breezes puff the ugly smog away from the immense basin, allowing, in the sun's brilliance, the encircling mountains and offshore islands to thrust boldly into view. Or the nights when after a winter rain sponges it clean the city—seen from a hilltop—is a vast, irregular checkerboard of twinkling squares studded with millions of tiny diamonds set against a background of black velvet. The view at night from a jet, which daily land by the hundreds at one of the busiest confluences of space-age travel, Los Angeles International Airport, is even more striking.

The many separate coastal cities, even such populous ones as Long Beach and Santa Monica, often seem mere seaside extensions of Los Angeles. Like the indeterminate seasons here, it often is difficult to tell where one town begins and another ends. But each is jealous of its identity and works to preserve it.

Long Beach, for instance, is an international port on a par with that of its big sister, Los Angeles. It also is a major U.S. naval base and a manufacturing hub, populated by a citizenry with an insatiable zest for sports, be they of the

Julia Pfeiffer Burns State Park

land or sea variety. For those who prefer water exertions, or simply sunbathing on the sand, the seven-mile arc of breakwater-protected beach is irresistible. And it is here off Long Beach that Great Britain's grand old luxury liner, the *Queen Mary,* rests at permanent anchor. The *Queen's* presence is testimony to Californians' ingenuity in manufacturing tourist attractions that match, in terms of profit, the state's endless natural ones.

San Pedro, the ocean end of a slender twenty-mile corridor extending from downtown Los Angeles and lined on either side by a chain of individual towns, actually is a limb of the supercity—the Port of Los Angeles on San Pedro Bay. Los Angeles annexed it about the turn of the century to provide itself with an outlet to the sea. The San Pedro breakwater, the Long Beach breakwater, and the middle breakwater between them almost spanning the bay are the world's longest, providing protection for the largest seaport complex in the Western Hemisphere—Los Angeles Harbor and adjoining Long Beach Harbor.

With its seafaring ambience and hilly streets, San Pedro probably is as distinctive a parcel of the city of Los Angeles as exists. Along the waterfront is an eye-catching complex of restaurants and import and specialty shops, some gotten up in the motif of an 1850s New England whaling village, the others patterned along post-Civil War California lines.

Its harbor is industrial, but, nevertheless, home to the West's biggest deep-sea fishing fleet and a popular departure point for sports fishermen. Terminal Island, largely man-made, between Los Angeles and Long Beach, is the chief wharf area for the twin harbors' deepwater craft.

Past San Pedro rises a great green headland, the Palos Verdes Peninsula. Eons past, this bulbous protrusion of shoreline (*palos verdes* means ''green sticks'') was an island. Today it is dotted with homes of those wealthy enough to build away from the dense urban crush, in neighborhoods like Rolling Hills Estates and Palos Verdes Estates. Views of the Pacific from here are without parallel in the Los Angeles metropolitan area. Beneath its sheer sea cliffs are beaches unlike others in the region, being merely short, rocky ledges along a series of coves. They are no place to sunbathe, and the boiling surf is no place to swim, but they delight tide-pool fanciers. Because of the concealment the coves afford, they once were the haunt of smugglers.

From Palos Verdes Point, at the peninsula's tip, a viewer can look south and take in the great sweep of the blue Pacific. Or gaze north to glittering Santa Monica Bay, with its curving shoreline, and the beads of cities strung one against the other in between.

Millions of people from other parts of the country have gotten their first sight of the Pacific from the sea edge of Santa Monica's flowery, grassy, palm-shaded Palisades Park, only one of the pleasures of this quiet, graceful old city. Knifing into the water from the south end of the park is one of the last of the grand old ocean piers. Although many another beach city has its fishing platform, Santa Monica's probably is the noblest of them all, with its cozy restaurants and snack stands, souvenir shops and fish markets.

At the northern outskirts of Santa Monica, the stark, slide-scarred Pacific Palisades mark the beginning of a sweep of high bluffs that vault westerly behind the shoreline. The Palisades are the seaward nubs of the Santa Monica Mountains, which have been sheared away by ages of erosion, to the distress of occupants of homes atop them. Almost annually, some new part of the cliff face crumbles, threatening to tumble residences, some of which already have cracked and broken apart, down onto busy Pacific Coast Highway and the broad beach just beyond.

The urban character of the populous shoreline ends with Malibu, where Mediterranean-style houses cling to slopes above the highway and other resi-

Big Sur

Garrapata Beach ▶

Point Sur

dences—some with streetfronts looking much like those of fishermen's shanties and others with elegant portals—hang over some of the most expensive beachfront in the world. For years, Malibu was the opulent lolling ground of Hollywood kings and queens, princes and princesses when the "star" system was at its apex, and many movie actors still maintain homes there.

The Los Angeles County coastline ends just above Point Dume, a bit bleak appearing after the glittering urban waterfront preceding it but with offshore rocks richly populated by cormorants and pelicans. This long, sheer-cliffed finger of sandstone points southward toward Santa Catalina, the most visited and most populous of the intriguing offshore Channel Islands.

The eight Channel Islands, ranging from ten to seventy miles offshore, lie roughly between Santa Barbara in the north and San Diego in the south. Except for magical Santa Catalina Island, with its storied resort town of Avalon, gemlike bay, and famed glass-bottomed boats, they are relatively unknown outside California. The islands are a treasury of protected plant and animal species, many of them rare, like the elephant seal.

The four southern islands are San Nicolas, San Clemente, Santa Barbara, and Santa Catalina. The northern group—San Miguel, Santa Rosa, Santa Cruz, and Anacapa—are known also as the Santa Barbara Islands.

The two largest islands, Santa Cruz and Santa Rosa, both are privately owned and, thus, comprise vast estates. On Santa Rosa are the only stands of Torrey pines, aside from those on the mesa north of San Diego which bears their name. The two smallest islands, Santa Barbara and Anacapa (actually a chain of three small islands), which is nearest the coast, were set aside in 1938 as a national monument.

Just west of Santa Rosa lies bleak San Miguel Island, its uninviting shores forbidden to civilian seacraft, since it is a target area for the navy's Pacific Missile Range. The remotest of the islands, San Nicolas, with communication and tracking instruments covering it, is the nerve center of the missile range and a vital adjunct to the big Point Mugu Missile Base lying perhaps seventy-five miles northeast of it.

From the Channel Islands back to the mainland is more than a distance of miles. It is a sea change from barrenness to settlement. Still, the navy's presence is felt in southern Ventura County just as inescapably as it is on the rocky isles of San Miguel and San Nicolas. The navy's interest in missilery is intense along the Point Mugu-Port Hueneme shoreline. The result has been the rapid growth, not only of the city of Ventura to the north but of towns slightly inland, including Oxnard, which calls itself the "Channel Islands City."

Ventura is a small city which developed around the still-existent relic of the Mission San Buenaventura, built in 1782 by that indefatigable architect of similar shrines, Father Serra, and since restored. The city nestles between the Pacific, incredibly blue here, and a lovely stretch of coastal range which includes mountains blanketed by pines and firs of lake-dimpled Los Padres National Forest, a huge preserve that embraces many peaks and valleys of southern California. Ventura's pride, among other things, is its luxuriantly soft climate and miles of handsome beaches, which are particularly appealing to surfers.

ABOUT TWENTY MILES north is proud, seductive Santa Barbara, almost everyone's enchanted city. It rises from a gently curling bay and ascends slopes which begin the foothills of the Santa Ynez Mountains, a range which crests sharply just back of and beyond the city. The mountain backlands are a wonderworld themselves. Their canyons and valleys are rich, rolling, oak-shaded pastureland and conceal from casual coastal travelers such surprises as the charming Danish town of Solvang and delicate Nojogui Falls, one of the most bewitching waterfalls in the state.

Modern Santa Barbara, a city with a noble and joyful past, occupies the site of what once was a substantial centuries-old Indian village. The Spanish explorer Sebastián Vizcaíno gave the place its name when he visited the area on December 4, 1602, the feast day of Saint Barbara. The presidio was established in 1782, and the "Queen of the Missions," with its unique twin towers and classical aspect, rose four years later where it stands restored today.

The altar light of the mission, the only one of the chain continually in the hands of Franciscan padres since its founding, has not snuffed out, it is claimed, since the dedication nearly 200 years ago. Some contend this faithful flame symbolizes the residents' resolve to preserve, even improve upon, the many still-existent reminders of Santa Barbara's Spanish legacy.

One of these is the castlelike county courthouse, a rambling, boldly ornate affair whose every cranny, from intricate iron work to frescoed ceiling, reflects Spanish grace. It frequently has been called the most beautiful public building in North America.

The red-tiled roofs and whitewashed walls of many homes and even the naming of certain streets for pioneer families, some of whose descendants still

Pinnacle Rock, Point Lobos Reserve

live in Santa Barbara, exhibit a determination to keep aglow the Spanish past. Evidence of this desire also can be seen in the exclusive suburb of Montecito, many of whose stone-walled, carefully landscaped, oak- and eucalyptus-umbrellaed old estates have survived the best-laid schemes of subdividers.

Palms grow along Santa Barbara's flowery waterfront abreast the main business district. This broad section of oceanside stretches from a smartly maintained yacht basin populated primarily by fishing boats and pleasure craft to a seven-acre lagoon. The still waters and grassy shores of this seaside pond constitute a refuge where thousands of birds—mallards and gulls, coots and blue herons, egrets and sandpipers—swoop and cackle.

While cool sea breezes cleanse the air almost every day, the ocean water temperature is agreeable and Santa Barbara rarely experiences a freeze. This benign climate encourages cultivation of great lemon groves, the lemon being one of the more tender fruits of the citrus family.

Arroyo Burro Beach Park, near the city's west limits, is a favorite of beachcombers. Below the cliffs there, one finds white-coated stones streaked with yellow and pale green which the experienced treasure hunter knows as the telltale indication of onyx. At low tide, the rocky headlands yield sea fossils.

The waters off Santa Barbara are not always the swimmers' paradise they would seem. In recent years, they frequently have been coated with oil resulting from spills and leakage from offshore drilling. Monster platforms, tall as twenty-story buildings, rise on long, steel legs in the federal tidelands of the Santa Barbara Channel where they support large derricks. Their presence has been a source of bitter controversy between environmentalists and the oil industry.

Goleta, just beyond Santa Barbara, is the site of a seaside campus of the giant University of California system. For some strange reason, it was named, not UC of Goleta, but UCSB—the University of California at Santa Barbara.

Lace lichen

Monterey cypress, Point Lobos

It also was at Goleta that the first vessel of substantial size to be built in California, a schooner designed for sea-otter hunting as well as coastal trade, was launched in 1830. Fittingly, *goleta* is Spanish for "schooner."

White bluffs above sandy beach become a characteristic of the coast as it spirals past what once was a famous landholding during the time of Spanish rule but which now is called Refugio Beach. In the days of the Spanish dons, it was the Ortega Rancho and took its name from a Lt. José Francisco de Ortega, among those present at the founding of Santa Barbara mission. That insatiable old rascal, the pirate Bouchard, plundered the rancho after sacking Monterey in 1818.

It generally is accepted that Gaviota, about twenty miles of climbing coastline above Goleta, represents the northern termination of the southern California coast. *Gaviota* is Spanish for "sea gull," birds which soldiers of the 1769 Gaspar de Portolá expedition observed here in such abundance.

The winding coast highway which has run close by, if not always along, the shore up to this point, now undergoes an abrupt change in character. It ducks through tunneling at windy Gaviota Pass and begins a long inland passage over rolling, oak-clad hill and through ranchland valley on which fat cattle graze.

The coastline changes too, becoming starker and far less inhabited as it sweeps directly west toward gale-buffeted Points Conception and Arguello where it angles almost ninety degrees straight north.

That tireless name giver Vizcaíno designated the so-called Cape Horn of the Pacific, the Punta de la Limpia Concepción in 1602, now shortened and anglicized to Point Conception. Well, anyway, that's one version. Another is re-

The Slot, Point Lobos Reserve

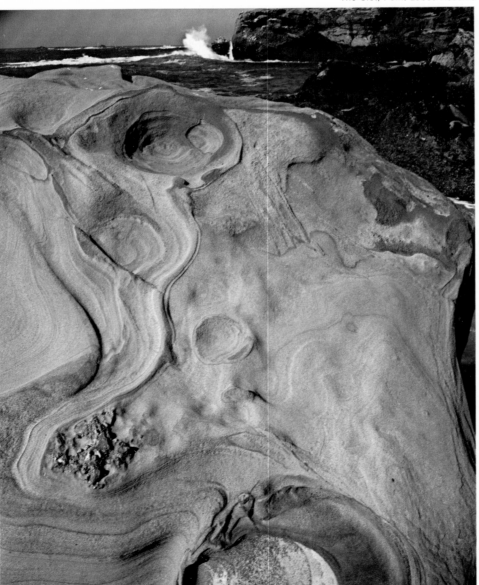

Cypress at Point Lobos Reserve

lated by William S. Murphy and Robert Kirsch in their fascinating book *West of the West,* and it bears on the naming of both Point Conception and Point Arguello. Knowing that Murphy, who did the bulk of the research, is an indefatigable browser among old manuscripts and letters, his and Kirsch's account strikes me as equally acceptable. Certainly, it is much more romantic and, if for no other reason, my preference. It tells of "California's most famous romance—the tragedy of the Doña Concepción Argüello," and it goes like this:

"When Georg Heinrich von Langsdorff, a Russian engineer who left an account of his visit, arrived in San Francisco on April 5, 1806, he was accompanied by Nikolai Rezanov, an official of the Russian American Fur Company. Negotiations to establish trade produced negligible results, as the colony was forbidden by law to engage in commerce with foreign vessels. For the Russians, this was a serious blow. Their settlement at Sitka, Alaska, was desperate for food. Something had to be done—and then Rezanov caught the eye of the military commander's daughter, Concepción Argüello.

"Langsdorff described her as 'distinguished for her vivacity . . . beautiful teeth . . . pleasing features, shapeliness of figure, and for a thousand other charms. . . .' Rezanov was duly smitten. He wasted no time in proposing, and the lovely Concepción accepted. The dour Langsdorff injects a callous note when he declared that his companion 'decided to sacrifice himself, by wedding Doña Concepción, to the welfare of his country, and to bind in friendly alliance both Spain and Russia.' Judging from his description of the girl's beauty, Rezanov's ardor could hardly have been motivated by patriotism.

"Concepción's parents found the Russian suitor unacceptable, his chief fault being that he was a member of the Orthodox faith. The distraught girl argued with her parents. She loved the handsome Nikolai. Moved by her tears, the Argüellos consented. It grieved them to surrender their daughter, who would sail away to a far-off land, but they had fourteen other children living in California to console them. A betrothal agreement was drawn up, but there was one stipulation: a consent for the marriage must be received from the Pope in Rome. Rezanov left for his homeland, vowing to return to his loved one. He never

Carmel-Monterey coast

Harbor seal

Point Pinos

Cormorants

reached his destination. En route, he fell from a horse, and died from the injuries he sustained. No one bothered to write Concepción. She moved to Santa Barbara, and, as legend says, maintained a lonely vigil, gazing seaward from a rocky point that bears her name, and where numerous vessels, including a squadron of United States Navy destroyers, have run aground in the fog that often drapes itself shroudlike along the coast. . . .

"Doña Concepción entered the Dominican Sisters' order on April 11, 1851. She received the name of María Dominga. She resided at their Benecia convent in the San Francisco Bay area until her death on December 23, 1857."

End of story. And so much for history or, perhaps, storybook stuff.

But it is an indisputable fact that the temperamental waters off the big land knob from which both points project are fraught with danger for mariners. Sometimes the sea runs placidly. But when the big blows arise, the waters churn and lashing whitecaps await like bounty hunters the unwary seafarer.

Raging seas, however, are only one of the perils. The other is fog, thickly camouflaging jagged rocks and other hazards behind her smoky skirts. It is from here on up that the fogs grow more impenetrable and occur more frequently as the California coast spirals toward Oregon.

But consider the other side of the coin. Here, the shore-bound fisherman encounters for the first time a creature that is a delicacy when fried but a squirmy worm of an object when netted: the smelt. The tasty little fish runs the summer surf from icy Alaskan waters to Point Conception, but rarely south of it. Ten inches long at most, the fish spawn in shallow tidewaters off sandy beaches beneath bluffs which ooze fresh water.

Smelt connoisseurs catch their prey by simply scooping them up with a variety of rakelike affairs, having nets at one end, when the beasties intrude on the water's edge before or after high tide, within a time span of perhaps no more than an hour either way.

Up the bluffy shoreline of ruggedly beguiling Purisima Point and Point Sal, rise vantages from which one can look northward over the Santa Maria Valley, back upon the coastal ridge, and inland to rippling hills occupied by Vandenberg Air Force Base. From Vandenberg are lobbed missiles and other space-age projectiles which streak the night sky and leave luminescent tracks visible for hundreds of miles.

Just inland too are the flower-growing town of Lompoc and neighboring La Purisima Mission.

Midway Point ▶

Lompoc is a blaze of color during the height of the blooming season, from late June through July—the colors of purple stock and bachelor buttons, Shasta daisies and poppies and marigolds. No other place in the nation equals Lompoc in the production of flower seeds, the chief industry of the town. More than 2,000 acres are sown annually and their yield, quite literally, is riches. An ounce of petunia seed is worth more than an ounce of gold. During the blooming season, the community attracts not only flower lovers but artists and color photographers by the scores.

La Purisima Mission, in Lompoc Valley, probably is the most completely restored of the 21 missions in the chain. It was founded in 1787, devastated by earthquake in 1812, rebuilt, then left to decay until Civilian Conservation Corps' crews undertook its restoration during the depression of the 1930s.

The coast highway exits from hill and dale at Pismo Beach, the name of a town that can hardly be forgotten once it's heard. Pismo Beach? That's correct. Pismo Beach, the clamming capital of California and home of the Pismo clam, a spectacular variety of that sweet-tasting shellfish. The largest known to have been dug from the sand here was a seven-inch monster weighing six pounds. If a clammer spades up one measuring less than four-and-one-half inches, state law requires that he rebury it.

Clamming is a sport, if that is the word, for everyone. All the clammer needs besides a $1 fishing license are dungarees and sneakers (or hip boots) and a rake, shovel, or spading fork with which to stab the sand. If he hears a clunk, the clammer knows he has scored. Pismo's is an ideal environment for the huge clams which thrive here, because its beach extends to one of the flatter under-water slopes on the coast, running a great distance before the water deepens.

Less well known than the clams as a Pismo attraction are the great swarms

Carmel coast

Cypress along Seventeen Mile Drive

of monarch butterflies that stop over here annually, arriving in November and staying through March, during a migration that takes the durable species all the way from Canada to Mexico. Some tagged by researchers have been found to have flown distances of 1,800 miles. They roost in Pismo's eucalyptus trees so thickly that the foliage appears to be yellow instead of green.

From Pismo Beach the highway, broad here and easily driven, dips inland again briefly, until it reaches San Luis Obispo, a historic county seat which reposes in a pretty valley extending to scenic Morro Bay about a dozen miles away on the coast. At San Luis Obispo, the northbound motorist must make a critical choice. He may choose the nonchallenging way and elect to drive U.S. Highway 101, fast and multilaned, up to the Bay Area. But if he does, he will miss some of the most dramatic seascapes in all the world, those along narrow, tortuous, and spine-tingling California Highway 1. For a short span, however—from San Luis Obispo west to the coast town of Morro Bay, then up to a point just north of the bay—California Highway 1 is multilaned.

Past the arc of San Luis Bay, on which Pismo Beach itself is situated, and the quaint old fishing villages of Avila Beach and Port San Luis in the sound's northern cup, the shore curves past bluffy headlands to a five-mile-long sandspit which points like a signaling finger at the largest natural monolith on the California coast: Morro Rock. It is, of course, no Gibraltar, but it is a natural wonder in its own right. It rises 576 feet and is almost completely surrounded by ocean water. Hordes of brown pelicans flock over it and occasionally a foolish fellow tries to climb it, to the distress of park rangers who must come to his rescue.

Morro Rock is the last of nine related peaks, cores of old volcanoes, which extend to the sea from San Luis Obispo. The little town of Morro Bay still is largely unspoiled, except for three giant cement stacks of a power plant which detract from its sparkle.

Past Morro Bay and extending to Carmel, the shore is an almost unbroken rocky shelf. Just past pine-cooled Cambria and neighboring San Simeon, coastal cliffs climb to precipitous heights where for long twisting miles on end the Santa Lucia Range crowds hard against the ocean, with sheer columns of stone plunging straight down into the whipping surf.

Cambria is a stunning little byway, strung along the banks of Santa Rosa Creek, its flanks hugged by piny hills and its face open to the ocean. Its pastoral amenities, although it is emerging as an artists' retreat, too often are ignored, especially by tourists rushing toward the twin spires of William Randolph Hearst's castle above the sea at San Simeon.

The opulent Hearst empire here once ran fifty miles along the coast and ten miles inland, and most of it, high undulating ranchland, was acquired by the late newspaper publisher's father, a onetime U.S. senator. The son began building his castle, La Casa Grande, and three guesthouses in 1919 and work

Fisherman's Wharf, Monterey

Martin's Beach, San Mateo

continued on it for more than a quarter of a century and at a cost of almost $50 million. The price does not seem all that outrageous, considering what splendor it bought. La Casa Grande was constructed mainly to house the art treasures which Hearst collected over a fifty-year period and on which he spent an estimated $1 million annually. Many parts of the castle, aside from the valuables it holds, were imported stone by stone and timber by timber from French chateau and Italian villa.

The 100-room castle—and it is a castle indeed—the guesthouses, the stables, and the exquisitely landscaped grounds on which grow more than 2,000 rose bushes, are astride a ridge overlooking little San Simeon, once a whaling village. The 123 acres of the original Hearst holdings now are a state historical monument, having been given to the state by the heirs in 1958. A half-million tourists arrive here each year to gawk at the baronial resplendence in which San Simeon's overlord once lived and entertained celebrities.

California Highway 1, which begins its precipitous ascendancy just beyond San Simeon, ribbons the steep, rugged coast most of the way to Carmel and conspires with the pounding surf below to lather with perspiration the palms of even the most nerveless motorist. It is no more than a coiling two-lane notch hacked from the face of the Santa Lucia cliffs. The riotous surf often is a sheer thousand feet below, roaring into cove after cove and slashing and clawing at already battered and broken rocks. Sometimes bridges carry the slender roadway across mountain canyons where deer scamper and brilliant wild flowers grow and fiercely flowing streams dash down to the sea past evergreen and eucalyptus.

The ocean here becomes a changeling, sometimes cobalt blue, sometimes emerald green, and sometimes even cloudy saffron, depending on the

depth of the water and the angle of the sun. Gulls soar and squawk along the stone pillars, sea lions bark from the misted worn rocks, and shy otters float through bobbing kelp beds.

This run of sinewy seashore from Morro Bay to Carmel is a sea-otter refuge. He is protected here within the ninety miles of coastal water which is his normal range because he has become so rare, even imperiled by extinction. Indeed, back in 1938, it was feared there were no more of these playful creatures, which yowl like a cat but which are relatives of the skunk, of all animals. Then a small herd was discovered off Monterey and, happily, its population continues to increase.

THE NORTHERN QUARTER of this steep-faced shoreline is a wildly splendid bleakness known as the Big Sur Country. It has been suggested that it is the last likely piece of geography in California to become populous because it is the dominion of those who prefer looking at the ocean rather than those who want to sport in it and along it. It was celebrated by dourly lyrical Robinson Jeffers in his narrative poems and has nourished the inspirations of generations of other writers and artists, including Henry Miller, who lived at Big Sur for nearly two decades.

Jeffers wrote of the meeting of surf and shore in such lines as:

". . . great waves awake and are drawn

Like smoking mountains bright from the west

And come and cover the cliff with white violent cleanness . . ."

Miller, observing that visitors see resemblances between Big Sur and other scenic splendors, protested that "comparisons are vain," and he wrote:

"Big Sur has a climate of its own and a character all its own. It is a region where extremes meet, a region where one is always conscious of weather, of space, of grandeur, and of eloquent silence. . . . On a clear, bright day, when the blue of the sea rivals the blue of the sky, one sees the hawk, the eagle, the buzzard soaring above the still, hushed canyons. In summer, when the fogs roll in, one can look down upon a sea of clouds floating listlessly above the ocean; they have the appearance, at times, of huge iridescent soap bubbles, over which, now and then, may be seen a double rainbow. . . .

Santa Cruz coast

Point San Pedro

"... Big Sur will be here forever, and perhaps in the year A.D. 2,000 the population may still number only a few hundred souls. Perhaps, like Andorra and Monaco, it will become a Republic all its own. Perhaps the dread invaders will not come from other parts of this continent but from across the ocean, as the American aborigines are said to have come. And if they do, it will not be in boats or airplanes.

"... Its mountain slopes are almost as treacherous as the icy sea in which, by the way, one scarcely ever sees a sail boat or a hardy swimmer, though one does occasionally spot a seal, an otter or a sperm whale. The sea, which looks so near and so tempting, is often difficult to reach. We know that the Conquistadores were unable to make their way along the coast, neither could they cut through the brush which covers the mountain slopes. An inviting land, but hard to conquer. It seeks to remain unspoiled, uninhabited by man.

"... Often, when the clouds pile up in the north and the sea is churned with white caps, I say to myself: 'This is the California that men dreamed of years ago, this is the Pacific that Balboa looked out on from the Peak of Darien, this is the face of the earth as the Creator intended it to look.' "

Millions of words have been written about the Sur country's haunting majesty, but hardly any improve on the acute grasp of it that Miller expressed in these passages.

Between Point Sur, a rocky node with a lighthouse partway down the seaward side, and Point Lobos, reaching like a many-fingered arm from the

Sand Hill Bluff, Santa Cruz

Santa Lucia Range into the ocean, the coastline gentles. The sea off it, however, becomes rougher, as contrary tides war with one another. Point Lobos itself is a battleground of natural forces which have produced its crowning glory, groves of gnarled and somber Monterey cypress.

The painter Francis McComas, a student of landscape, called this rocky promontory about five miles south of picturesque Carmel-by-the-Sea "the finest meeting of land and water in the world." The remark, like any other glorification, only invites contradiction, but it scarcely is without merit.

The Spanish named the headland for the herds of sea lions whose guttural yelps from offshore rocks which abound here can be heard great distances inland. *Punta de los Lobos Marinos,* they called it, "point of the sea wolves."

The twisted cypress, survivors of great geologic and biologic permutation, are making their last stand in a natural state on the high Point Lobos bluffs and at one other similar place just a short leap beyond: the western tip of the historic Monterey Peninsula. In this respect they are like the Torrey pines, which, to laymen, they resemble. The living cypress, with their rich green foliage and necklaces of lacy lichen clinging to them, stand, albeit bent and knobby, as an example of adaptability across cruel centuries, and they are beautiful. The fallen trunks and branches found here in profusion are beautiful too, with their surfaces bleached white and with orange red algae cleaving to them.

The moods of Point Lobos, a state protected reserve, are many. Sometimes violent and stormy. Sometimes peaceful and quiet. Sometimes vibrant and gay. The moods change with the season, weather, time of day, and presence or absence of fog. But almost all the time, Point Lobos is a place of ground color contrasting with the dark cypress foliage: the different green of fern and shrub, blue of lupine, yellow of buttercup, and red of Indian paintbrush.

Beyond Point Lobos, the Monterey Peninsula spreads fanlike out into the ocean. It is a hilly, wooded, enchanted land, and its communities, Carmel, Pacific Grove, and Monterey, are some of the most desirable in which to live, or play, along the California coast. The sparkling waters of Carmel Bay are to the south, and the sweep of Monterey Bay is to the north. The coastline of Del Monte Forest is one of the most spectacularly beautiful in the world, and a familiar sight to television viewers who also are golf fans. The peninsula's famous championship courses have been host to the great tournaments of the sport, and their treacherous natural hazards have challenged the best who play the game.

Sea lions

Natural Bridges State Park

76

Golf links are among the man-retouched scenic pleasures to be seen from the privately owned Seventeen Mile Drive, which curls from Carmel to the town of Pacific Grove, past fashionable estates, forested hills, and along ocean frontage wetted with dancing mists thrown up by the dash of whipped-cream breakers against the shore. The natural wonders are even more splendid. Of one of them, J. Smeaton Chase, a California writer who just before World War I traveled on horseback from Mexico to Oregon, wrote:

"At Cypress Point, the outer headland of the peninsula, where winds career most wildly, the gaunt wardens of the cliff have been torn, twisted, hunched, wrenched, battered, and hammered to the limit of tree resemblance. They make a Homeric-looking company, and tell a stirring tale of battle with

" '. . . every gust of rugged winds

That blows from off each beakéd promontory.' "

Carmel, often likened to an English seaside village, slopes through a pine wood to a beach of whitest sand. As early as the turn of the century, its thatched-cottage lure attracted artists and writers. Robinson Jeffers lived in Carmel. Today its galleries are an art fancier's treasure trove.

Despite growth and its allure for vacationers, Carmel remains pleasantly rural. Neither neon, streetlight, nor billboard is allowed. Sidewalks are permitted only along major commercial streets and, at almost all times of the year, are thick with tourists.

It is in Carmel, in Mission San Carlos Borromeo del Río Carmelo, with its five-foot-thick walls of golden limestone, that the bones of Father Serra lie. In 1770, the padre founded this now-faithfully restored church, as he did so many others in California.

Pacific Grove, like Pismo Beach more than 100 miles south, is visited yearly by swarms of monarch butterflies. Here their arrival is celebrated with an annual Butterfly Festival.

Monterey, it has been said, is a city with two different kinds of ghosts—those of Spanish explorers, governors, and missionaries and of Yankee sea-

Pescadero Beach State Park

farers and businessmen and those of a cast of equally real characters who people John Steinbeck's fiction, especially *Cannery Row.*

Monterey has preserved thirty adobe buildings that date from before the gold rush, giving the historic town a special allure. Some date back to the time when Monterey was the capital of Alta California—then under Mexican rule, including its oldest structure, the Custom House. The town had been the capital earlier—since 1775—when California was governed by Spain. The Old Custom House stands at the entrance of Monterey's Fisherman's Wharf, a jumble of buildings astride pilings which house restaurants, shops, and fish stalls.

Ironically, the old adobes today are more like the originals than Monterey's other special gift from history, Cannery Row, even though the latter is the relic of a less-distant past. It reached its peak in 1929, when its thirty canneries stretched along a roughly mile-long wharf and employed 4,000 people. Few fish-packing equals existed along the coast. Then, for some still-mysterious reason, the sardines disappeared from the Monterey coastal waters and never returned, and Cannery Row, as a viable commercial operation, died.

San Francisco

But the town lives on in the likes of Steinbeck's characters, Doc and Dora, Lee Chong and Mack—and the boys. He changed the names and manufactured a few, but most of the main ones were real, although, like the author, all now dead. Gone too are the old saloons and brothels and gambling halls which they knew and of which Steinbeck wrote.

Today, much of Cannery Row is a rusty, rotting, and empty sheet-iron canyon. Some of the old sardine-packing houses have been spruced up and revitalized as restaurants, art galleries, and shops.

Cabrillo, the prodigious discoverer, first sailed into Monterey Bay, but it was Vizcaíno who named it, after his patron, then viceroy of New Spain (Mexico), Count Monte Rey. The time was 1602, five years before the founding of Jamestown, a continent away.

Scant miles inland is vaster Steinbeck country, the long, almost straight Salinas Valley. The Salinas River cutting through the valley empties at mid-arc of curving Monterey Bay, just below the town of Castroville. The coastline of the bay is a sweep of broad white beaches, often indented by lagoons and beneath bluffs aburst, in their blooming time, with poppies and lupine. Above the bluffs are fields, often fog shrouded, where artichokes, that succulent, prickly delicacy, grow as they do no place else. Castroville, which was once the holding of a dis-

Japanese Tea Garden, Golden Gate Park

San Francisco Bay

San Francisco-Oakland Bay Bridge ▶

tinguished Spanish family, is, if you will, "the artichoke capital."

Just beyond is Moss Landing, whose lagoon once accommodated whalers and, later, a comparably exclusive strain of seafaring gambler, the rumrunner. Tales still are told in Moss Landing of pitched battles between liquor smugglers and federal agents during the lively, rapscallion days of Prohibition.

At the northern skirt of the bay is Santa Cruz, home to the most experimental branch of the University of California and a place where an old Franciscan mission has vanished (a half-sized replica has been built). Warm waters lap its broad beaches which are considered the safest along the coast. Hundreds of privately owned cottages and cabins line the shore, many available for rent or lease to family groups to whom Santa Cruz, with its spotless beaches and humming boardwalk, candidly caters.

Back of the Santa Cruz steppe rises a redwood forest whose trees are taller but not as husky as those of the giant sequoias of the Sierra Nevada. Mingled among the redwoods are stands of spruce and alder, bay and maple—through which sprint friendly deer.

Just north of Santa Cruz' pleasant beaches, the compatibility of sea and shore seems to change. Waves froth and fume, whittling away with brutal artistry at a slender, curving blade of sandstone which they have scalloped and perforated into arches. These are the much-photographed natural bridges of Santa Cruz.

Monterey Bay is now behind the northbound traveler on California Highway 1. He finds himself overlooking on the left a sweep of snowy sea beyond a great curvature of bluff and broad beach, sometimes pebbly but more often sandy, and occasionally chinked with blue green coves. On the right, passing from Santa Cruz County into San Mateo County—and even before—the landscape is a mural of lush farms with sea-weathered old barns and wooden homes against a background of soft mountainside.

As he continues north, the traveler motors through an occasional hamlet but no town of any size until he reaches Half Moon Bay. The town proper is about a half-mile inland from the lovely emerald and blue bay. From the tip of the bay, the coast, here mainly sandy beach below sandstone bluff—which ranges from just above sea level to heights of 100 feet—curves northeasterly, then runs straight north toward San Francisco.

Fisherman's Wharf, San Francisco

Eucalyptus, Marin County

FEW CITIES, and certainly none in North America, have been more sung about or written about than the sorceress by the bay. Bret Harte, one of the earliest—but by no means the first—to hymn her praises, wrote: "Serene, indifferent to Fate, thou sittest by the Western gate." Catchy sounding, but still fairly dignified, compared to the efforts of later lyricists, who, bent on eclipsing one another in encomiums, frequently ended in being unabashedly maudlin. But make no mistake: San Francisco is one hell of a town, really that place where, as Tony Bennett sings, one leaves his heart.

The City. That is what San Francisco Bay Area residents call it. And a special kind of a city it is. "A world-city," a writer who fell under its spell suggested, explaining: "In all cosmopolitan America, there's no place more cosmopolitan, none more distinctive. It is a truly American community, yet set down within it are colonies of alien peoples. Here where the sturdy spirit of the Argonauts still survives, you may hear on the streets a strange medley of tongues. 'Little Italy' clings to the slopes on Telegraph Hill and nearby are the bazaars of Chinatown. Each foreign quarter has its own quaint customs, and to eat of the cuisine of every nation in San Francisco's restaurants is to make a gustatory tour of the world." Although this was written more than twenty-five years ago, it still holds true—except that San Francisco's restaurants, though considerably more expensive, are better than ever.

More than any place else in the nation, to my way of thinking, San Francisco has to be seen, heard, smelled, touched, and even sensed to be really appreciated. Thus, no amount of, or even all the language that has been devoted to extolling the city truly captures San Francisco and its ambient bay region pleasures.

The first English visitors (Spaniards likely touched here earlier), that well-traveled privateer-cum-explorer, Sir Francis Drake, and his little company of men, didn't think much of the place.

The prospect of plunder drew Drake to the California coast in 1579. He had

set sail two years earlier from Plymouth Harbor, specifically commissioned by Queen Elizabeth I to "annoy the King of Spain in his Indies." But it was merely to repair the *Golden Hind* that Drake anchored the galleon hereabouts, most believe in a bay just north of San Francisco that bears his name today. Scholars disagree about where precisely Drake moored his ship. The issue was not settled when, under a rock in Marin County in 1936, a motorist found a plaque on which was an inscription, signed "Francis Drake," that claimed the area for England.

Some scholars suspect the plaque to have been a hoaxer's doing. In any event, after little more than a summer's month, Drake and crew hoisted anchor. The Crown apparently was not impressed by whatever reports it may have received regarding what Drake called "Nova Albion," for Great Britain made no attempt to colonize it.

Not the least, by far, of San Francisco's bewitchments is its weather. Moderate temperatures, comparatively warm in winter and relatively cool in summer, sustain the boast of some that the city lives in "eternal springtime." Thermometer readings seldom fall below fifty degrees or rise above seventy. During the last 100 years of record keeping, readings have climbed to ninety degrees or higher on an average of only once a year.

More exhilarating are the moods which descend on the city as a result of the interplay of climate and setting: ocean and bay and valley and mountain, around and beyond.

San Francisco sparkles like a magic white city when crisp breezes dance over the hills on sun-brightened days. The jutting skyline, with soaring new buildings that many traditionalists dislike, pierces the brilliant blue. Houses, many of them bay windowed, muted old masterpieces and others stucco-faced and gaily washed either pastel or white, glint in layers against the steep hills, often appearing to be hanging on for dear life to the narrow lots on which they were built and to the neighbors against which they crowd.

On such shimmering, sea-scented days, which are characteristic—few large cities in the United States have more hours of sunshine—one appreciates why San Francisco is called by some "the tilted city." One realizes too how densely settled it is, unmatched in the nation in that respect except for New York City.

Douglas iris

Muir Woods National Monument

Muir Woods National Monument

But sparkle, glint, shimmer, and clean blue sky give way on a late summer afternoon or early summer evening to the fabled San Francisco fog.

It does not creep in here on little cat feet; rather, it steals in on lion's paws. Great, cottony fluffs of mist surge through the Golden Gate, envelop the towers and trusses of the mighty bridge, spread across the bay, and bank against the hills, not just the San Francisco hills but those of Oakland, Berkeley, and the myriad other bay cities and towns.

Then sidewalks slicken, and the mood is the fog mood, soft and seemingly sound absorbent. But it does not muffle the clink-clank-clunk of the perky little cable cars crawling over the hills of the City.

The phenomenon results from saturated air moving over colder ocean water surfaces until the moisture condenses into fog or low-lying stratus clouds which the winds from the sea carry inland. Usually, the mists evaporate during the next midmorning.

San Francisco itself, packed along the knob end of the forty-mile-long peninsula of the same name, has a population of only about 680,000. And there is just about no way to crowd many more people in. But the San Francisco metropolitan area, running all the way south to San Jose just below the formation of the peninsula, has a population of more than 4 million. Strung along all sides of San Francisco Bay are, not only a thickly peopled suburbia, but cities of substance in their own right, especially those of the East Bay: Oakland (no longer that place of which Gertrude Stein said "there is no there there"), Berkeley, and Alameda. The San Francisco-Oakland Bay Bridge, eight miles long with its approaches, connects the major East and West Bay cities.

The jewel of Oakland is Lake Merritt with its grassy parkland, an oasis in midcity encircled by hotels, museums, and apartment and business buildings, which the lake waters mirror. Berkeley, of course, is the site of the main campus of the University of California system.

Northward from San Francisco, across the Golden Gate Bridge, beneath which ply vessels from the world over, travelers—and commuters by the thou-

Redwood sorrel

sands who use it daily—enter different territory. Some describe its flavor as bucolic or pastoral. Fair enough, perhaps. But Marin County is not rube's country. Anything but. The North Bay region, and certainly its communities with the most distinctive character, is largely populated by sophisticates, many of whom work in San Francisco while residing in exclusive and comely suburbs such as Mill Valley and Tiburon. Some live too in Sausalito which, however, is much more touristy and a haven for nonconformists, yet the picture-book equal of any of the Marin County communities. Sausalito rambles down a hillside to the bay's edge where one encounters an intriguing jumble of art galleries, homes on stilts, inviting shops and restaurants and, moored along the shore, houseboats and yachts.

Higher up, at the foot of Mount Tamalpais—the highest peak in the Bay Area and a great spot to watch the fog ooze across the water or view the glitter of San Francisco at night—is a cathedrallike grove of mighty redwoods. Muir Woods National Monument, less than twenty miles from the bustle of the city, is the last stand of the giant ancients in the Bay Area where once they thrived.

The coast along Marin County is a zigzag of cove and bay, including Drakes Bay. Here, just beyond a suburban fringe of cosmopolitan San Francisco, begins the majestic northern coast of California.

A ROVER traveling north beyond the San Francisco Bay empire's outposts suddenly perceives himself in a region of altered aspect. California Highway 1, which resumes its coiling thrust up the coast, runs along a shoreline wholly unlike that of the mostly placid and playful one of southern California, either in temperament or ornament. While the two-lane roadway is not so treacherous as that at Big Sur, it weaves and bobs from dizzying height to valley and back to dizzying height. Towns and cities

Ironstone ridges, Point Reyes National Seashore

Drakes Bay

Portuguese Beach

decrease in size, and settlements become more distant from one another.

The northern coast is a region of great stillnesses and often of loneliness. It is a region of rolling fog, sometimes high and ominous, sometimes scudding barely above ground level. It is a land of dark forests with rivers running smoothly and swiftly through them down to the crashing breakers which explode in great white plumes against the resisting cliffs. Often the mountains march straight down to the sea here. Occasionally sandy beaches and coves along which fisherfolk live interrupt the forbidding coastline.

It is a region of weather- and element-bleached ranch houses, barns, and wood-sided old stores, many with the look of New England about them. It is a region of abandoned and some still-existent lumber towns. These sprang up because of the Douglas firs which grow down to the ocean and because of the presence just slightly inland of redwoods, trees which thrive on the northern coast's prevailing dampness. Some of the lofty redwoods are nearly as old as Western civilization, but their number has been grievously thinned by the lumber industry. Fortunately, there are splendid specimens in government-protected parklands. The redwoods are the northern coast's treasure, shared with no other region, except where they overlap a short way across the Oregon boundary.

Despite fog and frequent rain, lashing surf and extended corridors of bleakness, the region has much to offer. The people themselves have a small-town friendliness. The resort and recreational centers have been constructed to take advantage of the environment. And on clear, sunshiny days, when the mists and fog stay behind their battlements at sea, the air has a special tingle.

About thirty-five miles northwest of San Francisco is one of the coast's most spectacular land reaches into the sea, Point Reyes. The rocky outcropping has a lighthouse and weather station at the tip. The weather station is the foggiest and windiest between Mexico and Canada. It is an even bet that on any given summer's day the steep rocky tip, more than 600 sheer feet above the inaccessible water's edge, will be fogbound, and on any day of the year, that gusts will be blowing off the sea up to forty miles an hour. The peninsula is an oddly shaped

Starfish

landmass, with not one, but two, arms flung into the ocean. The southern arm juts between the ocean and the long, curving sweep of Drakes Bay, with its flat, sandy beachlands; the northern arm, more of a splinter, between the ocean and the gently rippling waters of Tomales Bay, which knifes several miles southeast between peninsula and mainland. The unusual formation of land and water is the direct result of centuries of activity by the San Andreas Fault, which runs down the middle of Tomales Bay. Along this narrow inlet the mainland stretch is a mild and warm contrast to blustery Point Reyes. California Highway 1 here runs past pleasant pockets of beach on one side and meadowland on the other until it reaches Bodega Bay.

Bodega Bay, just into Sonoma County, is a pleasing commercial and sports-fishing town. Bodega is the name of a headland, a harbor, a bay, and a small community several miles inland. The Bodega region and the area north of it today

Salt Point State Park

attract more and more summer homeseekers and thus, more and more land developers. The townspeople like Bodega Bay the way it is and are unhappy over the turn of events.

Past the town of Bodega Bay, California Highway 1, in conformance with the snaky coastline it follows, spirals and dips and sharply ascends. Beneath high cliffs, the seas are wild and the land becomes one of bleak beauty. This once was Russian territory.

A sparkling river which empties into the ocean near Jenner, a resort town, today is called Russian River, but it was known to czarist adventurers as *Slavianka* —"the charming little one." Present-day inhabitants can assure you, however, that it isn't always charming. In recent years the river has overrun its banks in costly flooding.

The principal Russian settlement on the California coast was Fort Ross, thirteen miles north of the river, and thirty north of Bodega Bay, where the czar also had an outpost. The Russians built the fort on the site of a Pomo Indian

Sonoma coast

village overlooking a small harbor. In 1812, ninety-five Russian colonists and forty Aleuts from Russia's Alaskan colony began erecting a stockade of redwood. They took five years to complete the settlement and the two-acre fortification. But, once finished, it became a permanent base from which the Russian American Company carried on a fur trade and replenished the inadequate food supplies of its Alaskan colony.

But when California's sea-otter population became depleted to the point of near extinction, and the fort couldn't survive by agriculture alone, the czar ordered the colonists home. Captain John A. Sutter of gold rush fame bought the property, shipping everything that could be dismantled to New Helvetia (now Sacramento). Structures which could not be removed crumbled in the 1906 earthquake, after which the state acquired Fort Ross. Some of the restored buildings were damaged by fire in the early 1970s. These should be reconstructed by 1974.

Scattered along fourteen breathtakingly beautiful miles of Sonoma County coast north of Fort Ross is a residential development of 5,200 acres with the most sophisticated and aesthetic dwellings found anywhere. This is Sea Ranch. No other development has been so carefully planned in respect to the environment. A visiting newspaperman observed: "A book of covenants rivals the Bible in length. Acres of undeveloped land allow you to enjoy the ocean, the brown barren hills (called gold by the natives), the bitter loneliness of the landscape." Sea Ranch homeowners may not paint their wooden residences, nor may they build swimming pools or exposed tennis courts; they must do nothing to interrupt the stark sweep of the setting. But Sea Ranch's some 300 homes are not for the thrifty. Several are in the $100,000 bracket, and one cost $200,000.

North of Sea Ranch, just inside the Mendocino County line, is one of the

Sonoma Coast Beach State Park

Poppy and lupine

Fort Ross (being restored after recent fire)

region's formerly bustling lumber towns, Gualala, now a quiet coastal community with a quaint old hotel. The Mendocino coast is a primitive one, bold and rocky and broken at intervals by narrow coastal plains, but mostly steep bluff and craggy headland separated by deep coves and pebbly beaches, with bursts of wild flowers to soften the ruggedness. The waters off the Mendocino coast and to the north are unrivaled salmon fisheries.

Rain is frequent in the region and the temperatures even. At Fort Bragg, the principal town in the county, the thermometer has never risen above ninety degrees nor fallen below twenty-four.

A major outcropping along this coast is Point Arena, a dramatic wave-swept headland with a powerful lighthouse. About twenty-five miles north of this land-mark, atop a windy, sea-sculptured bluff, is the much-admired town of Men-docino. It was built in the 1850s by New Englanders, and a visitor from the northeastern United States still feels at home in what once was a lumbering center but now is an art colony. Both seascape and the community itself lure many resident artists. The town is a cluster of Victorian carpentry and aged red-wood water towers which winter storm and summer fog have dyed gray white. One of the Gothic surprises found along its short, narrow streets is the 100-year-old Mendocino Hotel, still busily discharging its duties as an inn.

Fort Bragg, named for a Confederate general and Mexican War hero, originally was an army post, abandoned after the Civil War, then resettled in the late 1860s following the construction of a sawmill. Lumbering remains its prime industry. One of the three largest redwood mills in California employs a fifth of Fort Bragg's population of about 4,500. About four miles north of the town, an unusual beach of black sand runs along the coast.

California Highway 1 continues along level shores and high headlands, past salt marshes and tidal mud flats, hugging the ocean. Then, just north of Rock-port, it veers inland and upward toward the damp forests of Humboldt County, where the redwoods rise from a floor of sword ferns, rhododendron, wild ginger, and poison oak. The narrow road here curves through hushed forestland where sunlight often appears only in dapples and spears. The darkness hides elk and black bear. At a town called Leggett, California Highway 1 ends at a junction with U.S. 101. The road continuing north bears the signpost 101, but is known as the Redwood Highway. It too coils through lovely forestland. The motoring can be slow going because of logging trucks and tourists' campers trickily negotiating sharp bends.

Oak, Mendocino coast

Much of the Humboldt County shoreline, west of U.S. 101, once was known as the Unknown Coast, and it remains today one of the most unspoiled and, concomitantly, least visited coastal sections anywhere. One forty-mile stretch is the longest roadless section of the United States' Pacific littoral, aside from Alaska. Here, cedars, spruces, firs, and redwoods grow among beds of azaleas, cascara, manzanita, and snowbush. Here, bobcats screech and the sharp-shinned hawk flies. And here, at Cape Mendocino, California makes its western-most intrusion into the Pacific Ocean.

Curling through the dark inland forests, U.S. 101 emerges on the coast just south of the most populous city in northern California, whose name, Eureka (Greek for "I have found it!"), is the state motto. Eureka, old and proud of its past, early developed into a flourishing mini-metropolis peopled by seafarers,

Point Arena

Mendocino coast at Westport

Carson Mansion, Eureka

commercial fishermen, shipbuilders, and lumberjacks. In 1854, a soldier named Ulysses S. Grant from Galena, Illinois, was stationed here at Fort Humboldt, now a state historical monument.

Situated in redwood country, Eureka has a natural harbor, Humboldt Bay, which with Arcata Bay is fourteen miles long, nearly four miles wide in places, and protected from the flogging ocean surf by two sandbars. Beyond the latter are superb fishing waters, and nearby rivers abound in salmon and steelhead. So Eureka was an ideal setting for the two industries which still sustain it: commercial fishing and lumbering.

Despite a sense of burliness which this manly commerce brings to it, Eureka also has a delicate Victorian air. This results from its numerous elegant old homes, built when it was believed the more embellishment man put on his castle—turret, tower, gable, and hand carving—the more beautiful it became. It is said that more than 100 craftsmen at one time worked on the Carson Mansion, now a private club but once the home of a lumber tycoon.

The shoreline north to the rocky, black mass of Trinidad Head, which is visible for a great distance, is some of the rainiest, foggiest, and cloudiest in the state and a tumble of sand dunes and jagged ocean reefs. Hills crested with some of the finest remaining stands of redwoods press close to the sea. Many of the redwood groves now are government protected from lumbermen's saws, following a protracted dispute between conservationists and the industry.

Past Little River is a rocky hole about fifty feet back from the sea cliff and connecting with an underground cave through which the surf surges. Confined within the rocky squeeze, the waves literally explode and spew towers of spray as high as forty feet into the air. The phenomenon is known as the Blowhole.

Trinidad, an old fishing town sheltered by the nearly 400-foot-high mass of Trinidad Head, was a mere hamlet about a decade or so ago and still is uncrowded. But it has become increasingly popular with prosperous Eureka pro-

Mill Creek, Redwood National Park

fessional people willing to commute daily. A onetime whaling station, Trinidad enjoyed a boom as a camp town of about 3,000 persons during gold rush days. It also once was the seat of Klamath, a county which no longer exists.

From Trinidad, the coastal highway runs past beaches abundant with driftwood—as so many along the northern coast are—and skirts a series of big lagoons whose quiet waters are separated from those of the ocean by long spears of sand. The scenic village of Orick sits past the last of the lagoons at the mouth of sinuous Redwood Creek. Along the stream, from a verdant floor of moss and fern, grow some memorable sequoias. California's last remaining herd of wild Roosevelt elk roam through Prairie Creek State Park along the seacoast near the boundary of Humboldt and Del Norte counties.

Del Norte, the northwest corner of California, is blessed with soaring trees, spectacular streams, and superb hunting, and salmon and steelhead fishing. Del Norte means "of the north." The county is thinly populated, with Crescent City, its seat, the only incorporated municipality.

The southern part of Del Norte County is Klamath River country. The wide-flowing stream charges between high-forested banks through some of the most primitive wilderness in the nation, a land where only now the old-style hunter and trapper is giving ground to the California sportsman. But at its mouth, about one-quarter-of-a-mile wide, the stream gentles. Requa, a picturesque village, sits on the north bank of the river. It is an old salmon-fishing hub, and Indians still live within and around it.

The Del Norte Coast Redwoods State Park stretches along the shore between the river and Crescent City, about fifteen miles northwest of the mouth of the Klamath. This redwood belt runs, unlike any other, down to the rumpled con-

Rhododendron

Redwood National Park

tour of the coast; the giants even cling to the precipice edge in a contorted posture that imitates the gnarled cypresses of Point Lobos.

Crescent City lies on the broad arc of Crescent Bay, with its miles of handsome beachfront, where sport paler but hardier brethren of the golden southern California surfers. Historic Crescent City Lighthouse on Battery Point, now a museum, stands on a hummock which, at high tide, becomes an island just beyond the harbor's outer breakwater. Once, when it was young, just nine years built, the old beacon may have fallen down on the job. Probably, however, there was just no way of preventing the disaster that occurred on July 30, 1865, when the steamer *Brother Jonathan* struck an offshore reef and broke apart. Of the 232 passengers and crew, only 19 made it to shore. Many of the dead were buried in Crescent City's town cemetery, now known as Brother John Cemetery.

From the jut of Point Saint George at the north edge of the city, the coastline takes a northeastward bend along Pelican Bay toward the misty cliffs of Oregon, just twenty miles away.

And there in the mists it all ends—the California coast.

But, before it does, an eerie thing happens. A phenomenon that is almost symbolic.

The giant redwoods stop their march.

Del Norte coast

118

They flourish in Del Norte County as they do in few other places. They grow in this northwest nook of California to an average height of 200 to 300 feet and along a coastal strip between eighteen and thirty-five miles in width.

But, at the Oregon border, except for a scattered grove just inside it, the stately ancients just plain stop.

It is as if the redwoods are saying: If the California coast ends here, so do we, California's own special treasure.

Del Norte coast